The Scripture Challenge

Lisa Toney

WIPF & STOCK · Eugene, Oregon

Barb
Rock your
world
for
Jesus!

Lisa Toney

THE SCRIPTURE CHALLENGE
Learn it. Live it.

Wipf & Stock
An Imprint of Wipf and Stock Publishers
199 W. 8th Ave., Suite 3
Eugene, OR 97401

www.wipfandstock.com

PAPERBACK ISBN: 978-1-5326-6542-4
HARDCOVER ISBN: 978-1-5326-6543-1
EBOOK ISBN: 978-1-5326-6544-8

The Scripture Challenge is dedicated
to Zoe, Gus, Pax, and Eden.
May these bold and beautiful words of Scripture
always be your superpower.

Introduction

A coyote ate my memory. Well, he could have. Early morning walks in the dark with my friend put us eyeball to eyeball with a few coyotes. My superpower of talking to animals doesn't work until after I've had my coffee, so we were out of luck. Our tiny flashlights armed us with a powerful beam from two failing AA batteries.

Of course, as we jog-walked the trail, my friend and I knew we only needed to be able to outrun one another if that coyote decided we were breakfast. We're close like that. One of us could get away. After all, Jesus said to lay down your life for your friend..., and she loves Jesus a lot! She really should be the one to lay down her life to prove that love...especially amongst coyotes.

It was on Coyote Trail that my friend and I talked about the brilliance of Scripture. We recognized it is God's genius that helps us to make better decisions in our lives. God's truth helps us to be better parents, spouses, and friends. God basically helps us do life better.

As the sun came up, we talked about the brilliance and beauty of these ancient words. God's Words are powerful and poetic...memorable even. Except not so memorable in our brains. We just couldn't seem to memorize them. *That*, friends, might just be impossible.

That coyote hasn't eaten my memory yet, but something has. Actually, many things have. My brain cells have been donated to lots of great causes. Some have been killed off. Some have been lost. Some snuck away when I wasn't looking. They gave up. Too many things were bouncing around up there for them to have any traction. Some just plain walked away. My brain cells have abandoned me!

So it is completely logical that I could not memorize Scripture. Other people could, but not me. My kids could because they still have shiny new brains. Their brain cells pump iron and do handstands. New languages? Sure. Coding? Check. Technology integration? No problem. My kids practice memorizing Scripture verses. They could do it. I could not. Lame. I mean, why even bother when we can instantly access Scripture on an app? Or read the pages of our Bibles? Guttenberg really rocked that printing press.

My friend and I pondered this dilemma while we walk-jogged amongst the coyotes. And right then and there, is where *The Scripture Challenge* was born.

We pinky-sweared while we ran the trail, okay, not really. We pinky-sweared while we *walked* the trail that we were going to try to memorize one Scripture each week. We were taking action. No more allowing brain cells to escape. Close the hatch and reconvene the party. The remaining few were given a pep talk and rallied. They had a new mission, a new purpose, a new calling...Scripture memorization.

Now, it is true, it could have been the early morning hour that prompted this madness. After all, I had not had my morning coffee yet, so anything is possible. With many important and worthy things to invest in, why would I risk the loss of my precious few remaining brain cells on this endeavor? Excellent question.

I need God. I need God like I need air. The more days I live and the crazier our world gets, the more I need God's strength, God's hope, and God's mighty power in my life. I need God's brilliance to speak into my brain. I need God's wisdom to wash over my wayward heart. I need Jesus not only in my heart, but in my mind, and in my words. Jesus is my hope. Jesus is my rock. Jesus anchors my soul.

So we decided to hold on to those precious, life-altering words of God with all that we had. As an anchor holds a ship safe in port, so we too would we lean into the power of the Word. We would learn it. We would live it.

So, where to start? Mama didn't raise no fool. Let's start with the shortest verse in the Bible: *Jesus Wept.*

Yes! We've got this! It's centered on Jesus, it's raw, it's real, and it's powerful. Actually all of that is true, but we didn't really start there.

When I did ask God to show me where to start, He led me to an unexpected place. Habakkuk. No, you are good; that is not a typo. This tiny little book in the middle of your Bible, is part of a collection of books called the Minor Prophets. I didn't think it was minor, though. God led me to a verse of major impact. Ready? Here it is:

Lord, I have heard of your fame. I stand in awe of your great deeds. Lord, repeat them in our day. In our time, make them known. In wrath, remember mercy.   Habakkuk 3:2

Brilliant, right? Powerful. Profound. Poetic. Helpful. A perfect place to start. And so we did.

We hit Coyote Trail early in the morning. We walk-jogged. (We still do not like to run.) But when we get out there, even before our coffee, we talk about life and faith. We watch the sun come up and we practice our Scripture. Sometimes she gets it. Sometimes I get it. Sometimes we both do and then we high-five and happy dance - if we are not crawling at this point.

Scripture memorization is a lost art. It is a hidden treasure more valuable than gold. It is a legit superpower. Knowing these verses for yourself anytime and anywhere infuses your mind with God's brilliance and your heart with God's strength. That power is ready to help you navigate every situation that your day might bring. It is your emergency supplies go-bag.

Hey, I think this might even regenerate brain cells. If Jesus could feed 5,000 with two fish and five loaves, I have faith He can work a miracle with my few remaining brain cells.

Come on and join us. You can even take *The Scripture Challenge* from the safety of your own home and leave the coyotes to us. One verse a week. Learn it. Live it.

You can use a journal to practice your verses as you learn them. Say them, write them, sing them, draw them, dance them, craft them, exercise them, or...fill in the blank. How do you like to learn? What things do you like to do? Add these verses to the mix - your mix. There is no one-way to do this.

A journal is also an awesome place to spend some time with God, reflecting and writing about what these verses mean for your life. Learn it. Live it. Learning them is only half the battle. It might not even be the hardest part. ***Living*** them is the adventure.

How do these verses change your perspective? How do they impact your relationships? How do they reshape your responses? How do you *live* them? Write it all down. Process it with God. Share it with a friend. Let these words really impact you — shape you.

You can do this! Bring it. Join the movement. Join a generation who is committed to the brilliance and life-changing power of the Word of God. Learn it. Live it.

Why should I memorize scripture?
(*You are cra-cra!*)

I c4n't MEMORIZE scripture!

I know....*me too*! It's hard to memorize things. I mean really, why should I even bother? I can grab my phone and look up Scripture anytime. I can dust off my Bible and just look it up. I get it. We live in this unbelievable time where we have access. Access anytime. I can juggle my coffee, my phone, my breakfast, my tunes, get directions, and look up the weather - all while driving. Is that even legal? I can order anything anytime and have a drone drop it at my doorstep. Okay, not yet — but it is coming, right?

Maybe being inundated with access is what has caused us to get a little apathetic when it comes to learning Scripture. If I can look it up, why in the world should I put precious brain cells to work? I have a million other things to do. My tribe wants to eat. All the time. They have this weird thing about three meals a day — every day. Plus snacks. So many snacks. Netflix is calling. Groceries. Laundry. Work. Bills. Paperwork. Sleep is high on the list. I get it.

Back in the ancient of days, life was still demanding, but in different ways. Work and dinner prep and sleep were still on their lists. But they also had family faith stories built into their life rhythms... Gather 'round and let me tell you a story...

That was how Granddad always began. He would gather everyone around the flickering light of the candle. Settling into a cozy spot, everyone would get ready for story time. Granddad would begin to tell the stories of old with colorful detail, passion, and personality. Stories of the amazing faith of men and women kept us on the edge of our seat and were told over and over again. Stories of our faith, our heritage, and our people were passed down from generation to generation.

The oral tradition of reciting out loud the history and majesty of God's work was the original way that God's Word was experienced and learned. For centuries, the brilliance and beauty of Scripture was remembered and recounted by the practice of out-loud story telling.

When we learn Scripture so that we can say it out loud, we join with our ancient ancestors of faith in this timeless tradition. We engage with the words in a different way than when we read them. Saying the words out loud, rolling them around in our mouth, pronouncing them with our lips gives us the opportunity to proclaim them and make them our words, our truths. Our ears get in on the action too and we get to hear them said with our own voice. Our brains jump on board and all of the sudden our senses are engaged in a different way than simply reading the words with our eyes.

The orthodox Jewish tradition of physical movement when praying employs the entire body. It is a beautiful sight to behold. During prayer, standing, bowing, swaying, and various hand movements are all used. Other Christian traditions kneel, sit, lift their hands, or even lay prostrate on the floor. Engaging your senses is a way to more fully experience that which you are seeking to know - a way to know Scripture more wholly, more deeply, with all that you are.

> *Jesus replied: "Love the Lord your God with all your heart and with all your soul and with all your mind."*
>
> Matthew 22:37

Here's the thing. I bet you can tell me your home address, the name of your elementary teachers, and the exact fifteen-word description of your Starbucks order. Maybe, just maybe (and this could be pushing it) you might even know your own cell number. Too far? I know, smartphones are making us...well...not so smart sometimes. I can still tell you my grandmother's phone number I memorized when I was a kid and my parents' home phone number. That is about it.

Can you tell me how to get to the closest gas station from your house? Or could you describe where your favorite restaurant is? How about the plot of your favorite movie? Maybe you could even sing me the lyrics to your favorite song. Yep, you *have* memorized stuff. You are able! That old noggin is still crankin' it out. You *can* memorize.

You can memorize something that will make you better at life. It is brain cell investment!

I don't have TIME for this!

Christians who memorize Scripture were not exposed to gamma rays to give them the ability. Sorry, no cool radioactive spider bites. They don't even have photographic memories. People who commit to memorizing Scripture have found a way to challenge themselves to make it fun, simple, valuable, and workable in their lives.

It's go time. Will you choose this? I think you are in if you are reading this. Somewhere your soul is crying out for this.

You *can* do this. Don't spend a lot of time on it. You can memorize Scripture by being intentional for five minutes a day. But you do need a plan. When and where will this go down?

Every morning when you get up, read your memory verse, say it out loud, write it down. You can exercise to it, sing it, act it out, craft it, fold laundry, empty the dishwasher, or a zillion other things. Connect this practice with something you already do. That will help your brain cells engage.

Get excited. Get pumped about this. Get those endorphins flowing. Make it fun. Look forward to it. If you find a way to get excited about it, then you will have fun with it. If you have fun with it, you will *want* to do it. Maybe it would be awesome to do this together as a family at dinnertime. Or maybe it would make dishes and cleanup more fun if you work on this together. My kids like to work on their verses before they go to bed. I like to work on mine in the morning when I walk with a friend. There are lots of different options.

Pray about it. Ask Jesus to show you when, where, and how best to memorize a weekly Scripture.

And here's the thing - when you memorize Scripture, it does become *a superpower*. God is able to bring to mind those verses that you learn to help make your life better. God will use those verses to remind you how to make wise choices and treat people better.

By the power of the Holy Spirit, God will bring those words of truth to the forefront of your heart and mind right when you need them. When you have written God's Word on your heart, it protects you from the sneak attacks of the enemy. It will make your spirit strong. Scripture *is* a superpower.

The law of their God is in their hearts; their feet do not slip.
Psalm 37:31

kid stuff for sure...
I am too OLD to memorize.

Old dog new tricks and all. Nope, I'm not buying it. God doesn't retire people. God actually sees a lot of value and wisdom in those with seasoned life experience.

Is not wisdom found among the aged?
Does not long life bring understanding?

Job 12:12

God called Moses at the tender age of 80 to deliver the Israelites out of slavery. Moses died at 120 and was still capable; if it had not been for his disobedience, he would have marched God's people right into the Promised Land.

Joshua was likely between 68-78 when he led the people into the Promised Land. Anna, the prophetess, a widow, about 84, was the first evangelist to proclaim Jesus to others. Her age was not a hindrance; perhaps it even helped to clarify her priorities. Jesus was her motivation. Even at 84 she was compelled to say and do new things because of the power of Jesus in her life.

She gave thanks to God and spoke about the child to all who were looking forward to the redemption of Jerusalem.

Luke 2:38

why BOTHER?
what's in it for ME?

If you do this hard thing, there are some big wins in it for you. Really big wins. Are you tired of doing the things that you don't want to keep doing? Do you wish you could change? Do you want your life to be different? This is a big resource for you. This could be what you need to get things moving in a new direction. Know why? Because... This. Is. Powerful. That is why it is hard and daunting. Satan does not want you to do this because it gives you access to God's power. The enemy will fight you in this because he would much rather you stay where you are rather than see you move forward in strength and in the authority of God.

Memorizing scripture brings focus to your life. Memorizing verses will cause you to spend time directing your thoughts to the things that God wants for your life rather than the things that this world is pressuring you to do. When you need to make a decision, these words will spring to mind in just the right moment. God will use these words to guide you and protect you. The Spirit will use these truths to shape you to look more like Jesus. These words will make you better at life.

Scripture verses you can say with your mouth, head, and heart at anytime of the day or night, when you are facing any situation, can bring clarity and direction for how you should act. These words of truth and power can inform your decisions. If you want to know what God wants you to do, learn His words. Consider this an invitation from God. Each challenge verse gives you an opportunity to change how you live your life.

These words direct you to the One who gives you the power to fight off temptation. The words themselves are not magic. It is the God of these truths who holds the power. With these words, God can redirect your steps. God can move you to make a different decision. God can use these words to change how you respond to your marriage, to your kids, to your grandkids, to your parents and siblings, to your friendships, and your work and school relationships.

These are the most brilliant and beautiful words ever written. You are invited to this powerful wisdom word feast. Whaaaat? Access to *all*. No secret societies, no passwords, no education or experience needed. The mystery revealed. Isn't that rad? I love it!

God may even allow you the honor of introducing someone to Jesus because you know these words. When they are right on your tongue, God can show up in some pretty amazing ways in your life and use you to expand the Kingdom of God. You. That is right. You...doing Kingdom work! Don't miss out!

I'M IN.

How does The Scripture Challenge work?

Yaaaaas. You are in. Start the par-tee. High five. Fist bump. Happy dance. Props to you for accepting **The Scripture Challenge**. Are you ready? Here we gooooooo...This is going to be fun! Not like cake and presents fun, but important, big-deal life stuff fun.

God is going to show up for YOU. Awesomeness is going to happen. God is going to work in your life through these verses. Prepare for awe. You are not going to want to miss this. Write it down. Get a journal. I'm serious. If you don't write it down, it will be harder to remember what God wants to say and do in your life through these verses.

Here's the game plan:

On **Day One**, say that verse. What do like about it? What is interesting about it? What is your favorite part? Say the verse two or three times out loud. Write it out in your journal one or more times to practice saying it and writing it. You can even circle, highlight, or underline words. This is your journal and your time with God, so be as creative or as non-creative as you want! Ask God to help you to learn the verse and apply it to your life.

On **Day Two** say the verse out loud a couple of times. Then write the verse out a few times to practice learning it. Block phrases or words together with lines, arrows, and boxes to help you make connections to memorize it. Write out some thoughts about this verse. How can you apply it to your life today? Write out a prayer to God asking Him to reveal Himself to you in this verse.

On **Day Three**, see if you can write out the verse from memory. Yes, you can peek. No worries if you forget parts (or all of it). Don't get discouraged! You **can** do this! Spend some time journaling a prayer to God about the process of memorizing this Scripture and how God is using it in your life.

On **Day Four**, say the verse two times. Try to write the verse out from memory. Yep, you can still go back and look at it if you need to. No shame. No judgment here; we are rallying those brain cells; I totally get it. Be real with God in your journal. How are you seeing God show up in your life with this verse? Do you dare to invite God to change the way you talk, think, or act by the power of these profound words?

On **Day Five**, try to say it out loud and write out the verse from memory. How much of it could you get? I bet you have some of it down. You are a rock star. Great job. It is starting to flow. You are on your way to having this gem stored in you as a life treasure. Write out what this verse has meant to you as you have worked on it this week. What have you learned? Where has God challenged you? Have you noticed any changes in your words, thoughts, or actions? Write out a prayer to God inviting God to continue to use this verse in your life both now and in the future.

10

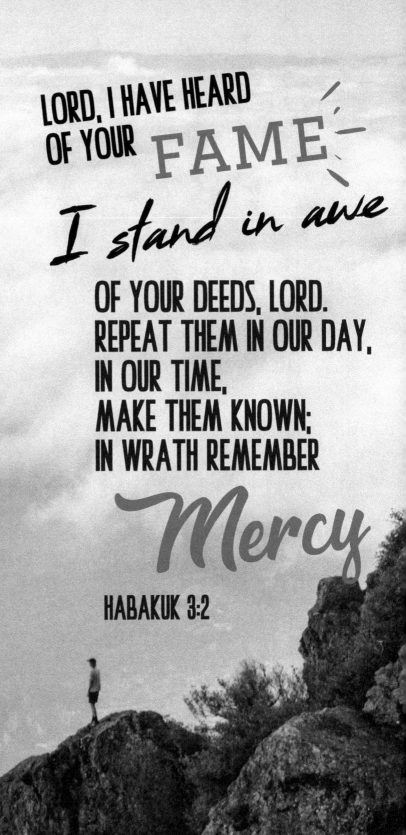

LORD, I HAVE HEARD OF YOUR **FAME**

I stand in awe

OF YOUR DEEDS, LORD.
REPEAT THEM IN OUR DAY,
IN OUR TIME,
MAKE THEM KNOWN;
IN WRATH REMEMBER

Mercy

HABAKUK 3:2

FOR I AM **CONV INCED**

THAT NEITHER DEATH NOR LIFE,
NEITHER ANGELS NOR DEMONS,
NEITHER THE PRESENT
NOR THE FUTURE,
NOR ANY POWERS,
NEITHER HEIGHT NOR DEPTH,
NOR ANYTHING ELSE IN ALL CREATION,

WILL BE ABLE TO SEPARATE US
FROM THE *love* ≪≪≪

OF GOD THAT IS IN
CHRIST JESUS OUR LORD.

ROMANS 8:38-39

02

MY SALVATION
AND MY HONOR
DEPEND ON GOD;
HE IS MY MIGHTY

RO
CK

MY REFUGE.
Trust in Him

AT ALL TIMES, O PEOPLE;
POUR OUT YOUR HEARTS
TO HIM, FOR GOD
IS OUR REFUGE.

PSALM 62:7-8

HAVE I NOT
COMMANDED YOU? BE

STRONG

and courageous

DO NOT BE TERRIFIED;
DO NOT BE DISCOURAGED,
FOR THE LORD
YOUR GOD
WILL BE WITH YOU

WHER
EVER

YOU GO.

JOSHUA 1:9

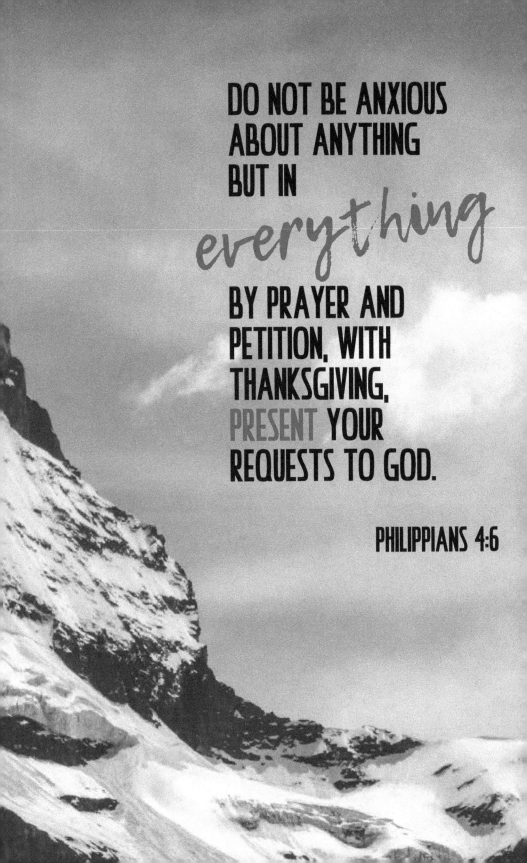

NOW CHOOSE
LIFE
SO THAT YOU
AND YOUR CHILDREN MAY LIVE
AND THAT YOU MAY LOVE
THE LORD YOUR GOD, LISTEN
TO HIS VOICE, AND HOLD FAST
TO HIM FOR THE LORD IS
YOUR
LIFE

DEUTERONOMY 30:19

The Lord

DOES NOT LOOK
AT THE THINGS
MAN LOOKS AT.

MAN LOOKS AT THE
OUTWARD APPEARANCE,
BUT THE LORD
LOOKS AT

THE HEART

I SAMUEL 16:7

BUT HE SAID TO ME,
"MY *grace*

IS SUFFICIENT FOR YOU,
FOR MY POWER
IS MADE PERFECT IN WEAKNESS.
THEREFORE I WILL BOAST
ALL THE MORE GLADLY ABOUT
MY WEAKNESS SO THAT CHRIST'S

POWER

MAY REST ON ME."

2 CORINTHIANS 12:9

Find Rest

O MY SOUL,
IN GOD ALONE;
MY HOPE COMES
FROM HIM.
HE ALONE IS
**MY
ROCK**
AND MY SALVATION;
HE IS MY FORTRESS,

*I will not
be shaken.*

PSALM 62:5-6

FOR YOU CREATED MY INMOST BEING.

you

KNIT ME TOGETHER
IN MY MOTHER'S WOMB.

I PRAISE YOU

BECAUSE I AM FEARFULLY AND
WONDERFULLY MADE;
YOUR WORKS ARE

wonderful

I KNOW THAT FULL WELL.

PSALM 139:13-14

DO
Everything
WITHOUT GRUMBLING
OR ARGUING,
SO THAT YOU MAY BECOME

blameless

& pure,

CHILDREN OF GOD
WITHOUT FAULT
IN A WARPED AND
CROOKED GENERATION.

PHILIPPIANS 2:14-15

YET THIS I CALL TO MIND
AND THEREFORE I HAVE

BECAUSE OF THE LORD'S
GREAT LOVE
WE ARE NOT CONSUMED,
FOR HIS COMPASSIONS
NEVER FAIL.
THEY ARE NEW
EVERY MORNING;

LAMENTATIONS 3:22-23

BUT WHOEVER LIVES BY

the Truth

COMES INTO

THE LIGHT

SO THAT IT MAY BE SEEN PLAINLY
THAT WHAT THEY HAVE DONE
HAS BEEN DONE
IN THE SIGHT OF GOD.

JOHN 3:21

15

Peace

I LEAVE WITH YOU
MY PEACE
I GIVE YOU.
I DO NOT GIVE TO YOU
AS THE WORLD GIVES.
DO NOT LET YOUR HEARTS BE
TROUBLED AND

DO NOT BE AFRAID.

JOHN 14:27

I HAVE TOLD YOU
THESE THINGS,
SO THAT IN ME
YOU MAY HAVE

peace

IN THIS WORLD
YOU WILL HAVE TROUBLE.
BUT TAKE HEART!

I HAVE
OVERCOME
THE WORLD!

JOHN 16:33

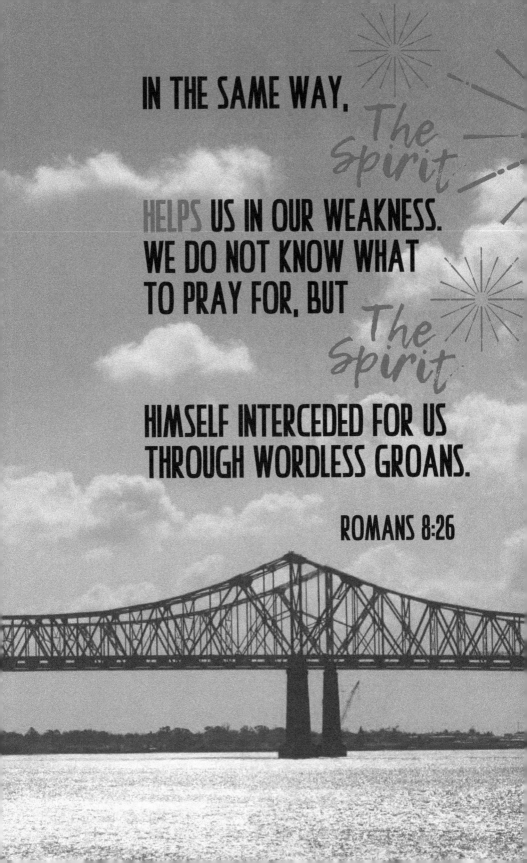

IN THE SAME WAY,

The Spirit

HELPS US IN OUR WEAKNESS. WE DO NOT KNOW WHAT TO PRAY FOR, BUT

The Spirit

HIMSELF INTERCEDED FOR US THROUGH WORDLESS GROANS.

ROMANS 8:26

CONSECRATE
YOURSELVES AND BE
Holy
BECAUSE I AM
THE LORD YOUR GOD.
KEEP MY DECREES
AND FOLLOW THEM.
I AM THE LORD,
WHO MAKES YOU
Holy

LEVITICUS 20:7

NEVER BE LACKING IN **ZEAL** BUT KEEP YOUR SPIRITUAL FERVOR SERVING THE LORD. BE JOYFUL IN HOPE PATIENT IN AFFLICTION, FAITHFUL IN PRAYER.

ROMANS 12:11-12

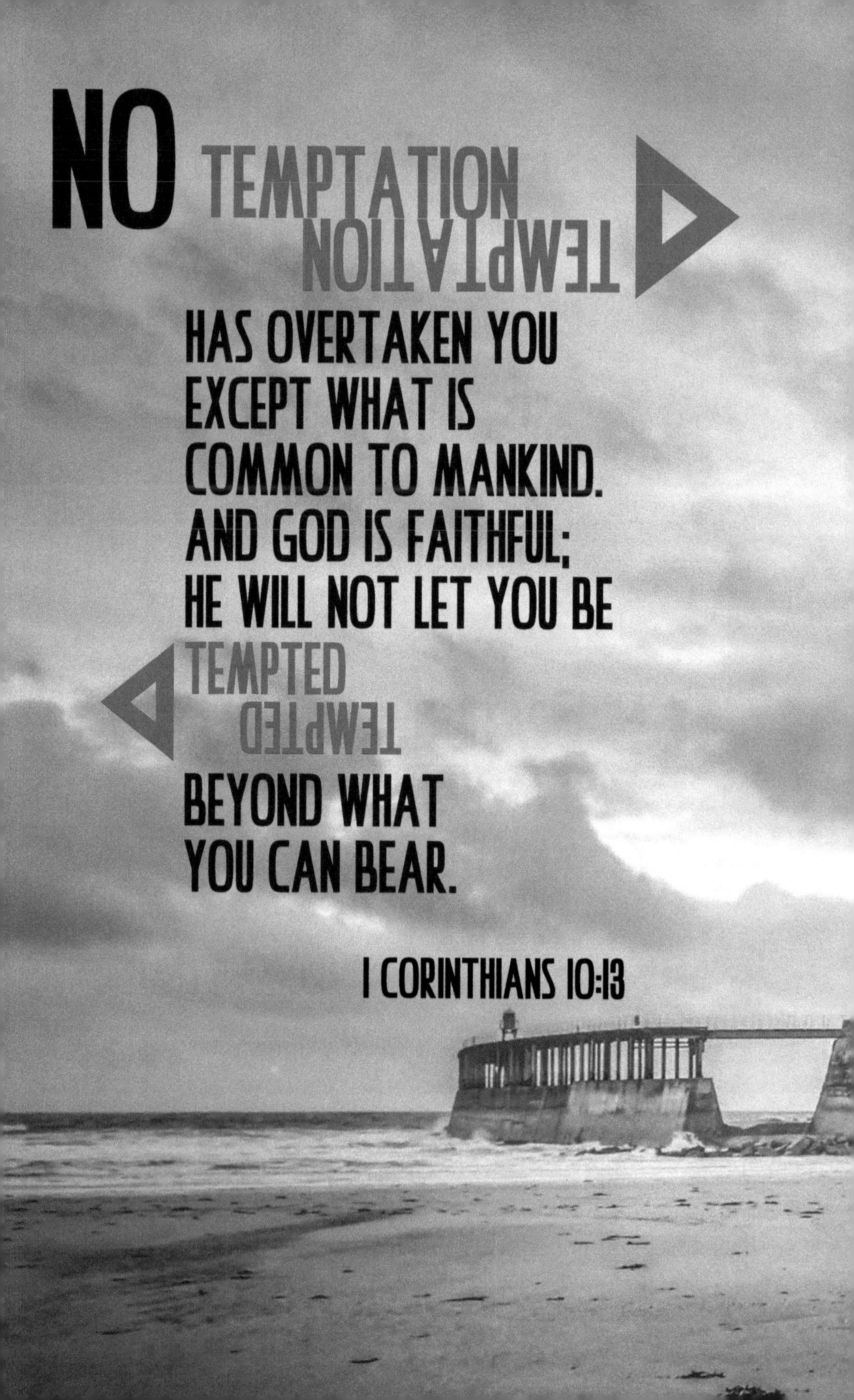

NO TEMPTATION
HAS OVERTAKEN YOU
EXCEPT WHAT IS
COMMON TO MANKIND.
AND GOD IS FAITHFUL;
HE WILL NOT LET YOU BE
TEMPTED
BEYOND WHAT
YOU CAN BEAR.
I CORINTHIANS 10:13

21

BUT WHEN
YOU ARE TEMPTED,
HE WILL ALSO
PROVIDE A **WAY**
OUT

SO THAT YOU CAN
STAND UP UNDER IT.

I CORINTHIANS 10:13

THE LORD YOUR GOD
IS WITH YOU,
HE IS MIGHTY TO SAVE.
HE WILL TAKE GREAT
DELIGHT IN YOU;

HE WILL QUIET YOU
WITH HIS

Love

HE WILL REJOICE
OVER YOU
WITH SINGING.

ZEPHANIAH 3:17

32

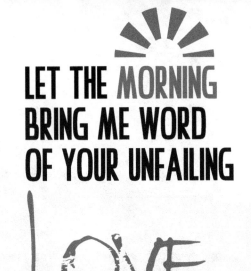

LET THE MORNING
BRING ME WORD
OF YOUR UNFAILING

LOVE

FOR I HAVE PUT
MY TRUST IN YOU.
SHOW ME THE WAY
I SHOULD GO,
FOR TO YOU
I ENTRUST MY LIFE.

PSALM 143:8

Rejoice

IN THE LORD ALWAYS. I WILL SAY IT AGAIN:

Rejoice

LET YOUR GENTLENESS BE EVIDENT TO ALL. THE LORD IS NEAR.

PHILIPPIANS 4:4-5

25

Love is...

PATIENT,
LOVE IS KIND.
IT DOES NOT ENVY,
IT DOES NOT BOAST,
IT IS NOT PROUD,
IT DOES NOT DISHONOR OTHERS,
IT IS NOT SELF-SEEKING,
IT IS NOT EASILY ANGERED,
IT KEEPS NO RECORD OF WRONG.

1 CORINTHIANS 13:4-5

LOVE

Love

DOES NOT DELIGHT IN
EVIL BUT REJOICES
WITH THE TRUTH. IT
ALWAYS PROTECTS,
ALWAYS TRUSTS,
ALWAYS HOPES,
ALWAYS PERSEVERES.

1 CORINTHIANS 13:6-7

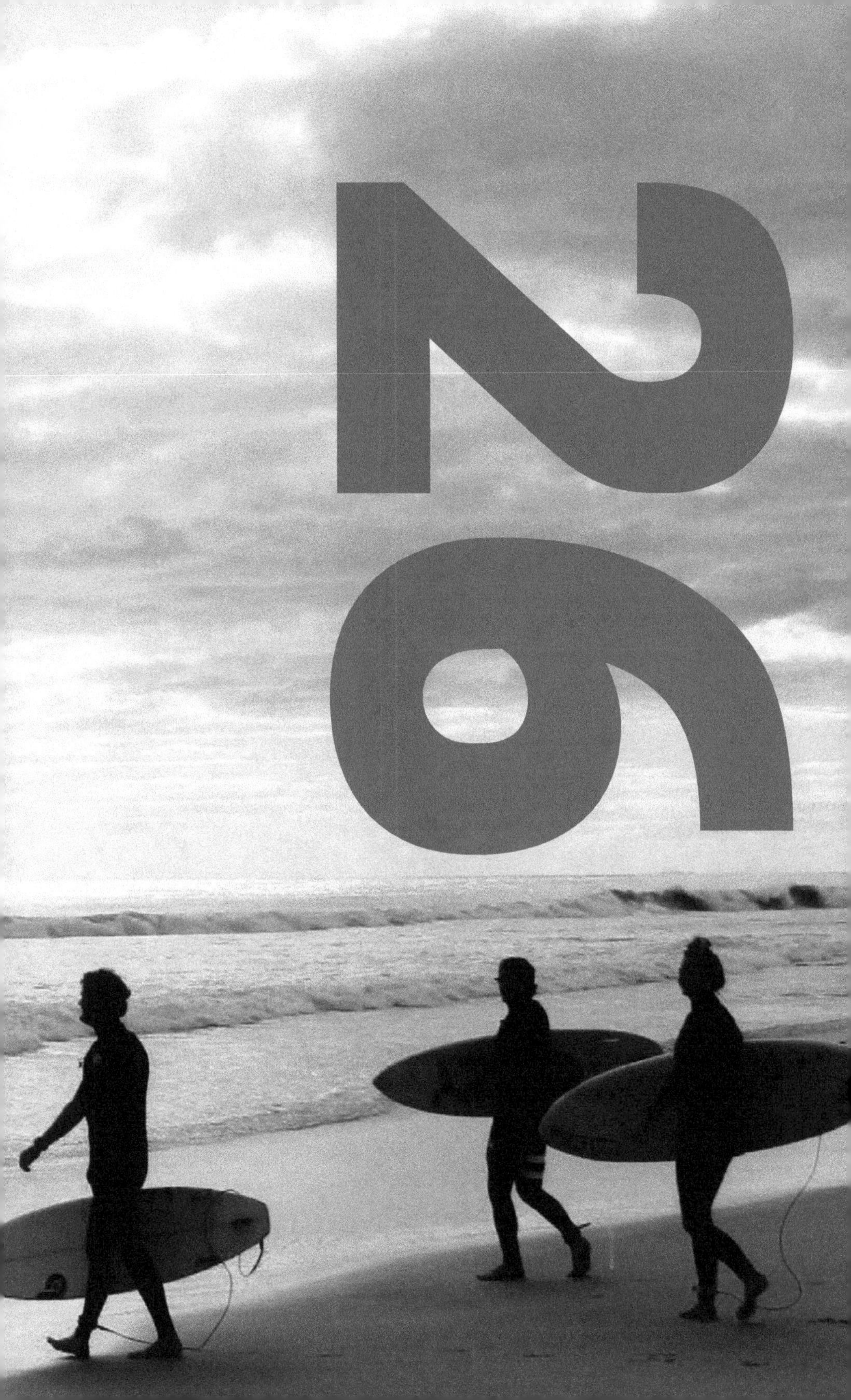
26

BE COMPLETELY HUMBLE
AND GENTLE;
BE PATIENT,
BEARING WITH ONE ANOTHER IN
love
MAKE EVERY EFFORT TO KEEP THE
PEACE
OF THE SPIRIT THROUGH
THE BOND OF
UNITY
EPHESIANS 4:2-3

FORGET

THE FORMER THINGS;
DO NOT DWELL ON THE PAST.

SEE I AM DOING A

New Thing!

NOW IT SPRINGS UP;
DO YOU NOT PERCEIVE IT?

ISAIAH 43:18-19

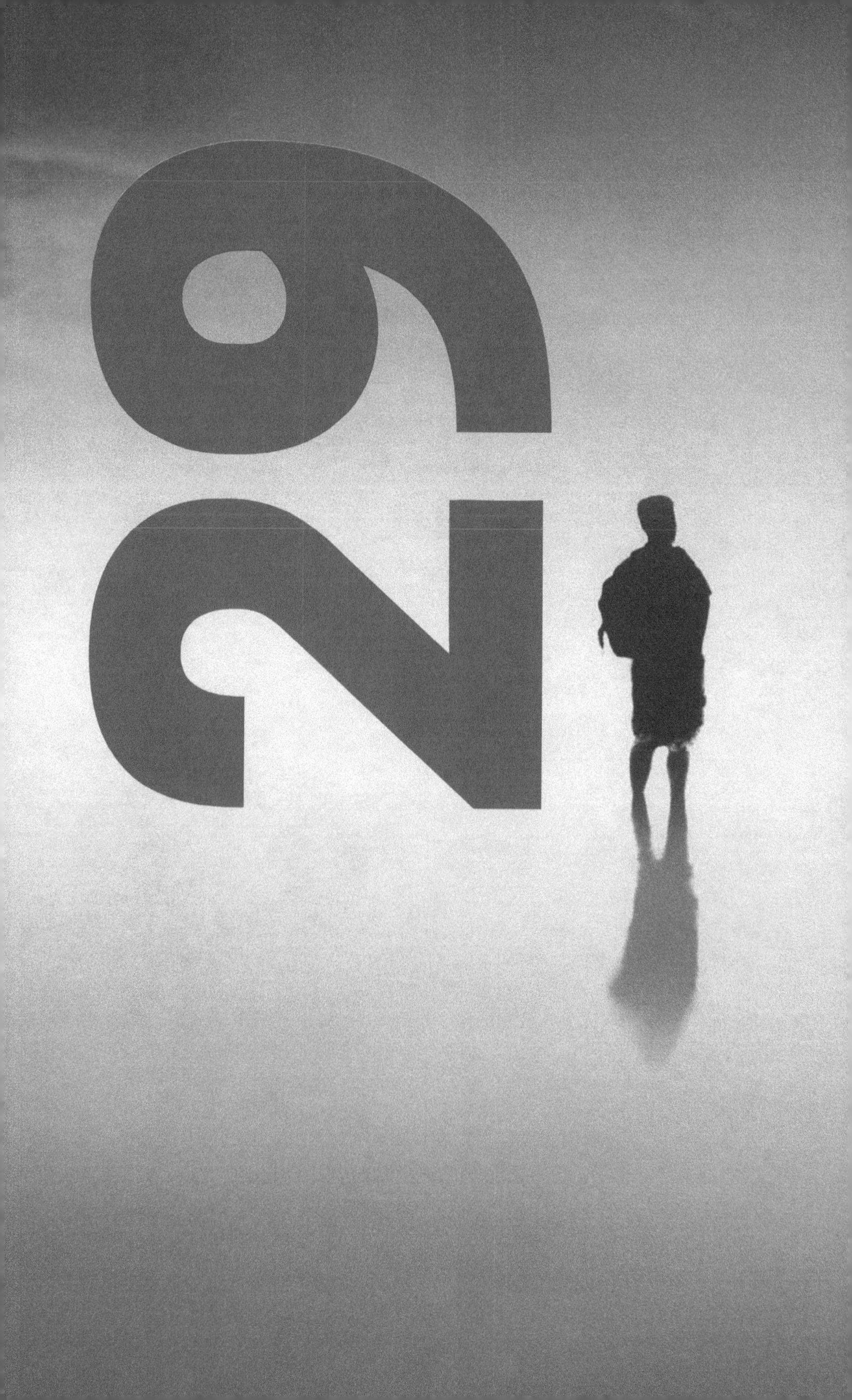

FINALLY, BE

STRONG

IN THE LORD
AND IN HIS MIGHTY POWER.
PUT ON THE FULL ARMOR OF GOD
SO THAT YOU CAN
TAKE YOUR STAND
AGAINST THE DEVIL'S SCHEMES.

EPHESIANS 6:10-11

STAND STRONG

DO NOT **CONFORM** ANY LONGER TO THE PATTERN OF THIS WORLD

BUT BE *transformed* BY THE RENEWING OF YOUR MIND.

THEN, YOU WILL BE ABLE TO TEST AND APPROVE WHAT **GOD'S WILL** IS

HIS GOOD, PLEASING, AND PERFECT WILL.

ROMANS 12:2

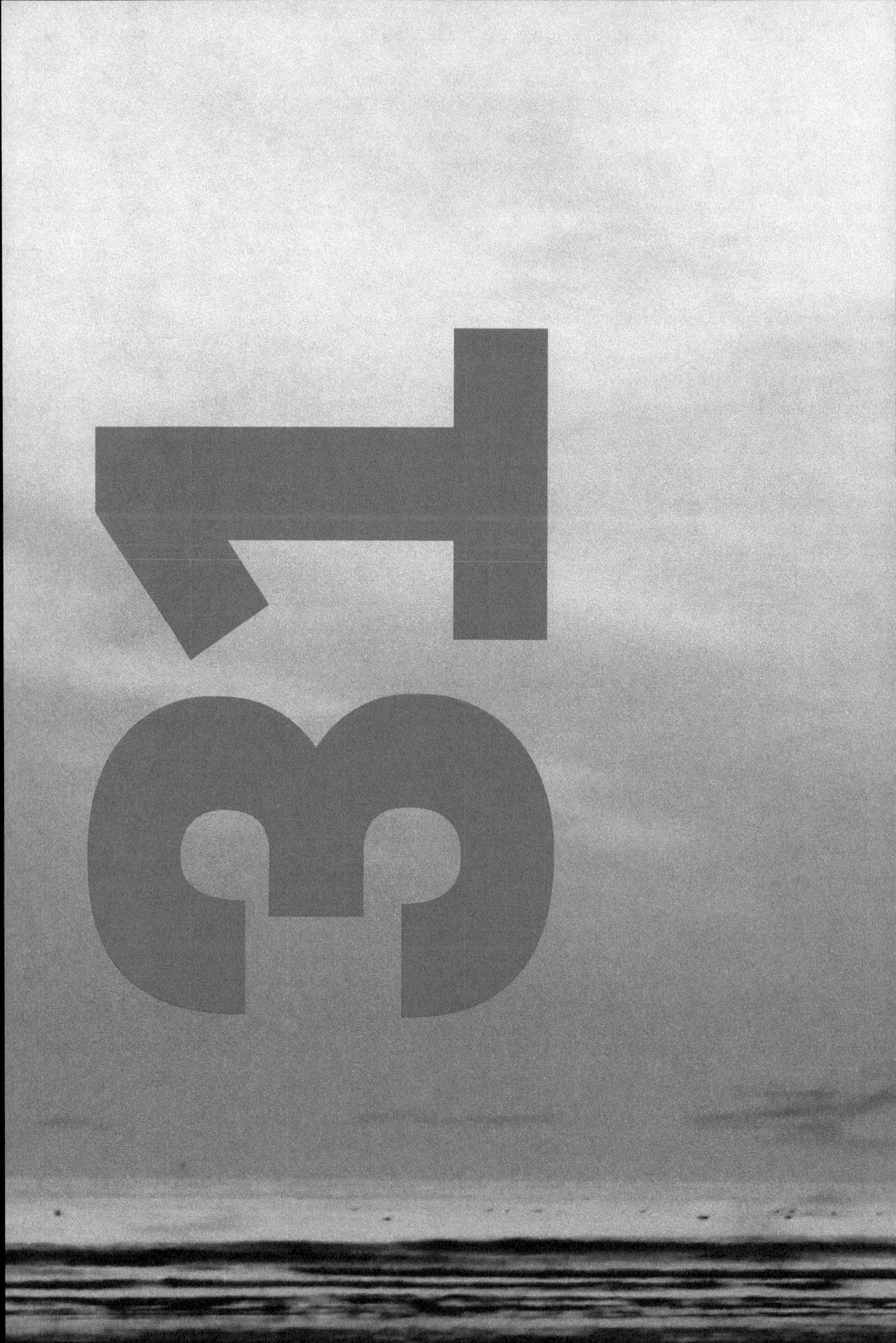
31

AND THE *peace* OF GOD, WHICH TRANSCENDS ALL UNDERSTANDING WILL

GUARD

YOUR HEARTS AND YOUR MINDS IN CHRIST JESUS.

PHILIPPIANS 4:7

FINALLY,
BROTHERS AND SISTERS
WHATEVER IS TRUE
WHATEVER IS PURE
WHATEVER IS LOVELY
WHATEVER IS ADMIRABLE
IF ANYTHING IS EXCELLENT
OR PRAISEWORTHY

think
about
such
things

PHILIPPIANS 4:8

32

whatever

YOU DO
WORK AT IT
WITH ALL YOUR HEART,

AS WORKING FOR THE LORD,
NOT FOR HUMAN MASTERS,
SINCE YOU KNOW
THAT YOU WILL RECEIVE
AN INHERITANCE FROM THE LORD
AS A REWARD.
IT IS THE LORD CHRIST
YOU ARE

serving

COLOSSIANS 3:23-24

Rejoice Always

PRAY CONTINUALLY;

GIVE THANKS

IN ALL CIRCUMSTANCES, FOR
THIS IS GOD'S WILL
FOR YOU IN CHRIST JESUS.

1 THESSALONIANS 5:16-18

35

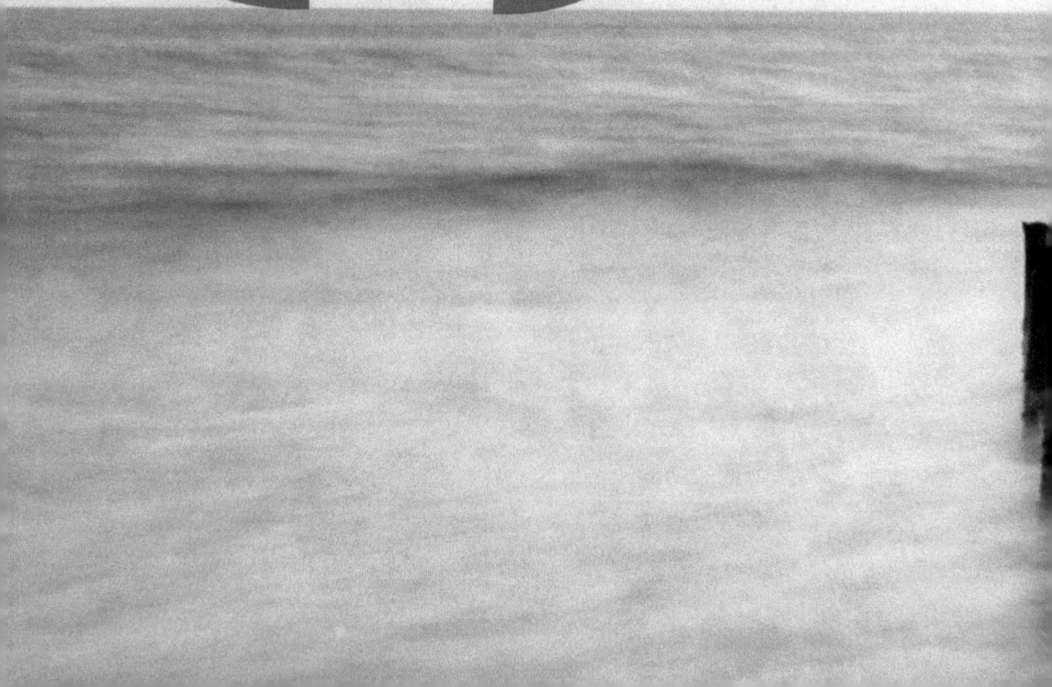

BUT THE LORD IS

faithful

AND HE WILL

STRENGTHEN

YOU FROM THE EVIL ONE.

2 THESSALONIANS 3:3

FOR THE SPIRIT
GOD GAVE US
DOES NOT MAKE US

timid

BUT GIVES US

POWER

LOVE,
AND
SELF-DISCIPLINE.

2 TIMOTHY 1:7

LET US THEN APPROACH
THE THRONE OF
GRACE
WITH CONFIDENCE
SO THAT WE
MAY RECEIVE MERCY
AND FIND GRACE
*to help us in our
time of need.*

HEBREWS 4:16

LET US FIX OUR EYES ON

Jesus

THE AUTHOR AND PERFECTOR
OF OUR FAITH, WHO FOR THE

J
O
Y

SET BEFORE HIM
ENDURED THE CROSS
SCORNING ITS SHAME,
AND SAT DOWN AT
THE RIGHT HAND OF
THE THRONE OF GOD.

HEBREWS 12:2

IF ANY OF YOU LACKS

WIS

YOU SHOULD
ASK GOD
WHO GIVES
GENEROUSLY

DOM

to All

WITHOUT
FINDING FAULT
AND IT WILL BE
GIVEN TO THEM.

JAMES 1:5

AND THEREFORE, WITH MINDS THAT ARE **ALERT** *and fully sober*

SET YOUR

ON THE GRACE TO BE BROUGHT TO YOU WHEN JESUS CHRIST IS REVEALED AT HIS COMING.

1 PETER 1:13

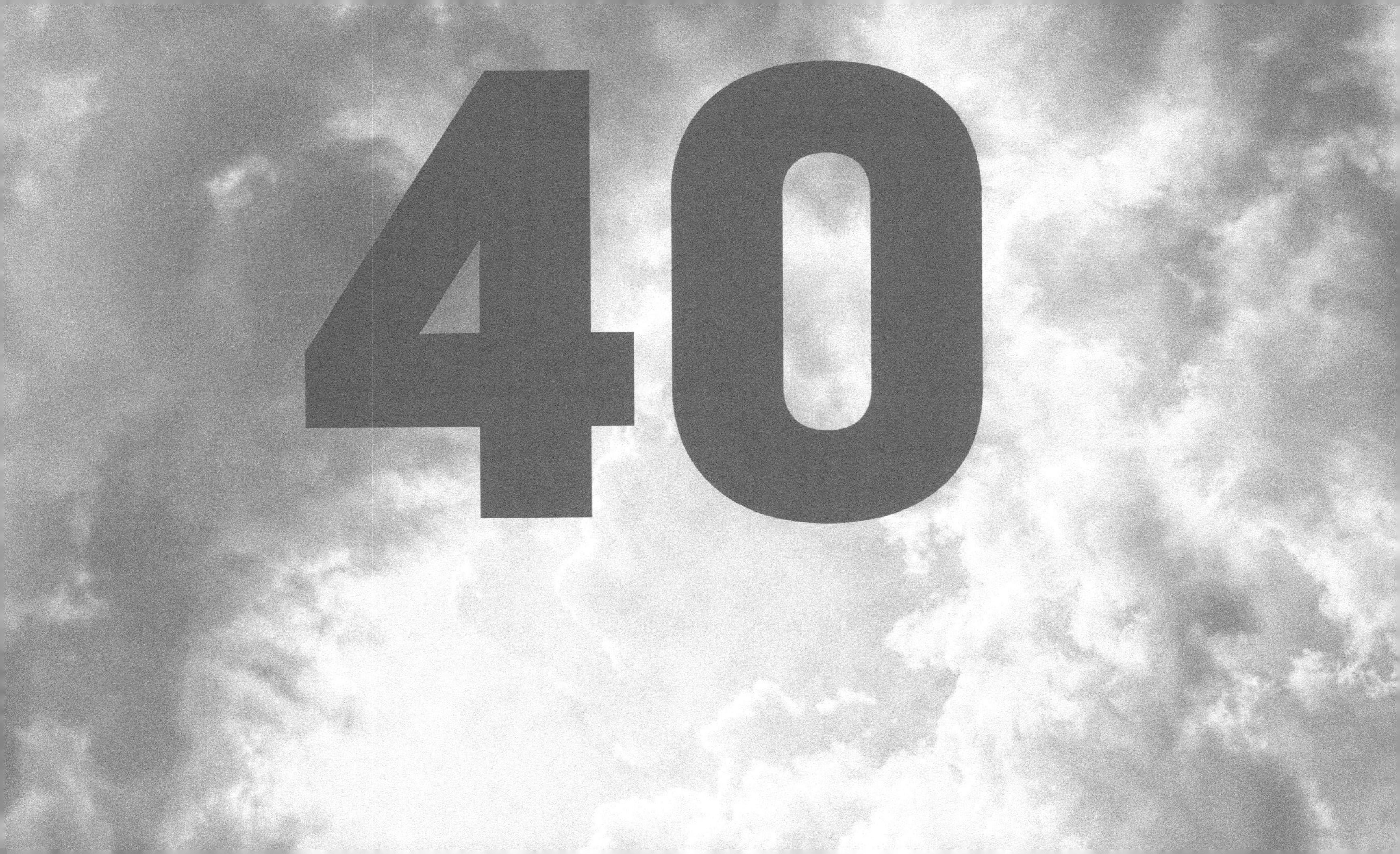
40

DO NOT REPAY
EVIL WITH EVIL
OR INSULT WITH INSULT,
BUT WITH

blessing

BECAUSE TO THIS
YOU WERE CALLED
SO THAT YOU MAY INHERIT A

blessing

1 PETER 3:9

IF YOU ARE
INSULTED
BECAUSE OF THE NAME
OF CHRIST YOU ARE
BLESSED FOR THE
Spirit of Glory
AND OF GOD
RESTS ON YOU.

1 PETER 4:14

HUMBLE

YOURSELVES, THEREFORE UNDER GOD'S *mighty* HAND, THAT HE MAY LIFT YOU UP IN DUE TIME. CAST ALL YOUR ANXIETY ON HIM BECAUSE HE CARES FOR YOU.

I PETER 5:6-7

BE *Alert* AND OF SOBER MIND. YOUR ENEMY THE DEVIL PROWLS AROUND LIKE A ROARING LION LOOKING FOR SOMEONE TO DEVOUR.

RESIST HIM

STANDING FIRM IN THE *Faith*

1 PETER 5:8-9A

HIS DIVINE POWER

HAS GIVEN US

everything

WE NEED FOR
LIFE AND GODLINESS

THROUGH OUR KNOWLEDGE OF HIM
WHO CALLED US
BY HIS OWN GLORY AND

goodness.

2 PETER 1:3

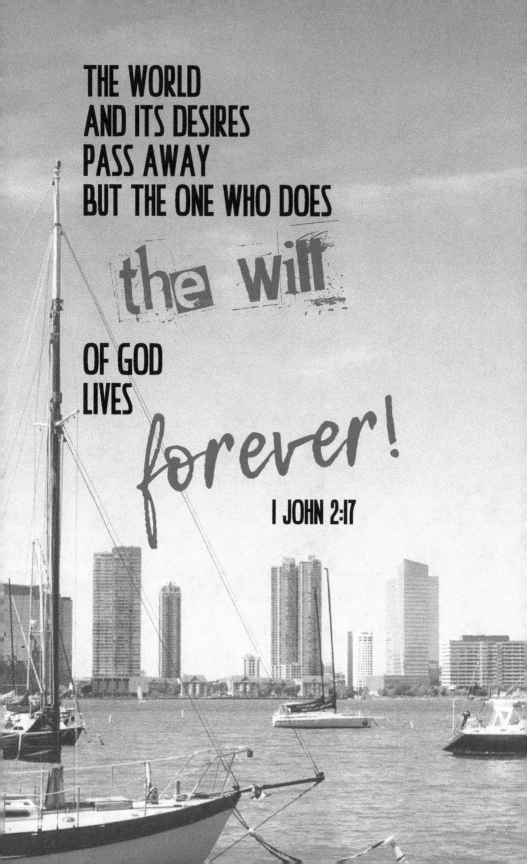

THE WORLD
AND ITS DESIRES
PASS AWAY
BUT THE ONE WHO DOES
the will
OF GOD
LIVES
forever!

1 JOHN 2:17

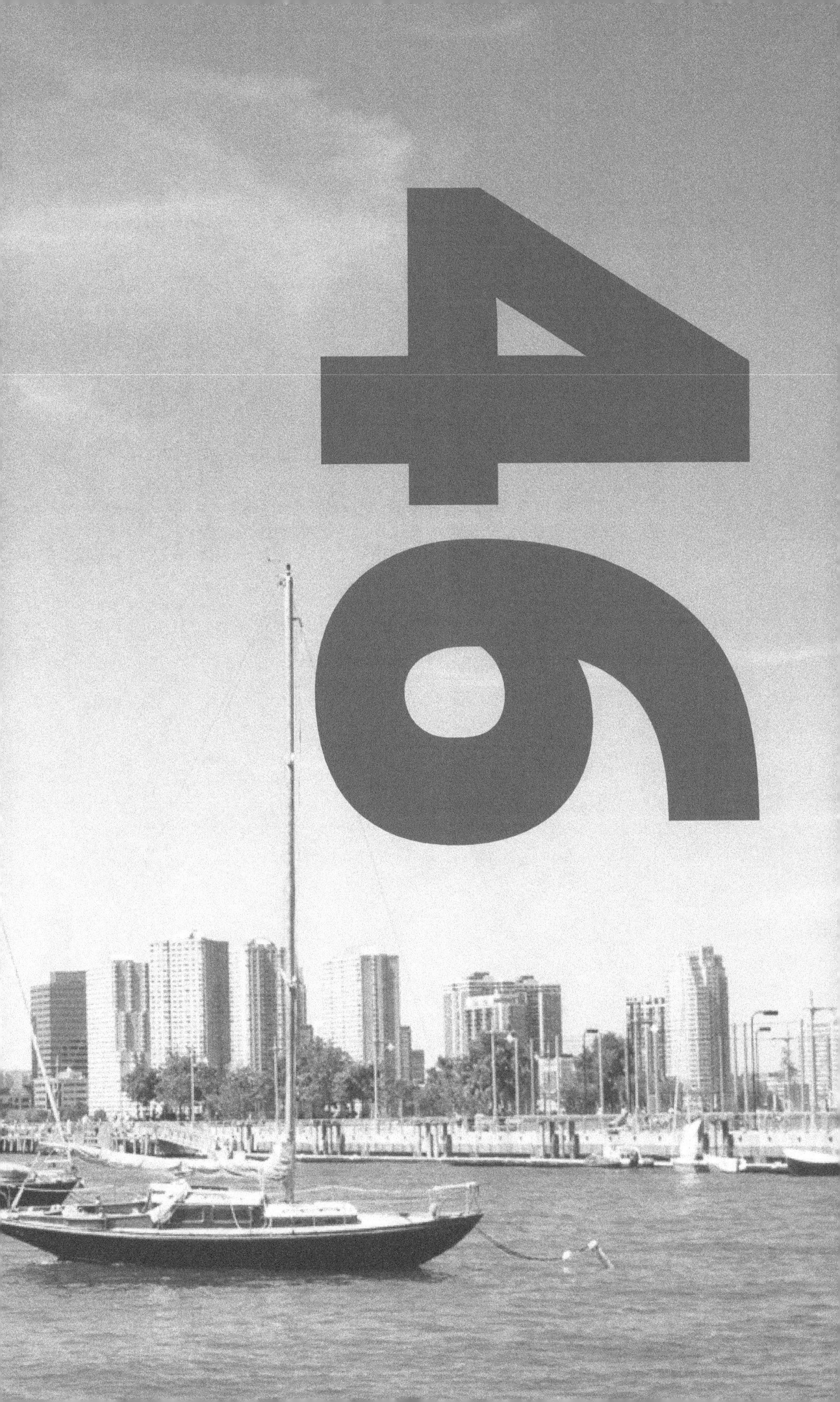
49

You
DEAR CHILDREN,
ARE FROM GOD

AND HAVE OVERCOME THEM,
BECAUSE THE ONE
WHO IS IN YOU IS

GREATER

THAN THE ONE
WHO IS THE WORLD.

I JOHN 4:4

THIS IS THE

confidence

THAT WE HAVE
APPROACHING GOD:
THAT IF WE ASK

ANYTHING

ACCORDING TO HIS WILL, HE
HEARS US.

I JOHN 5:14

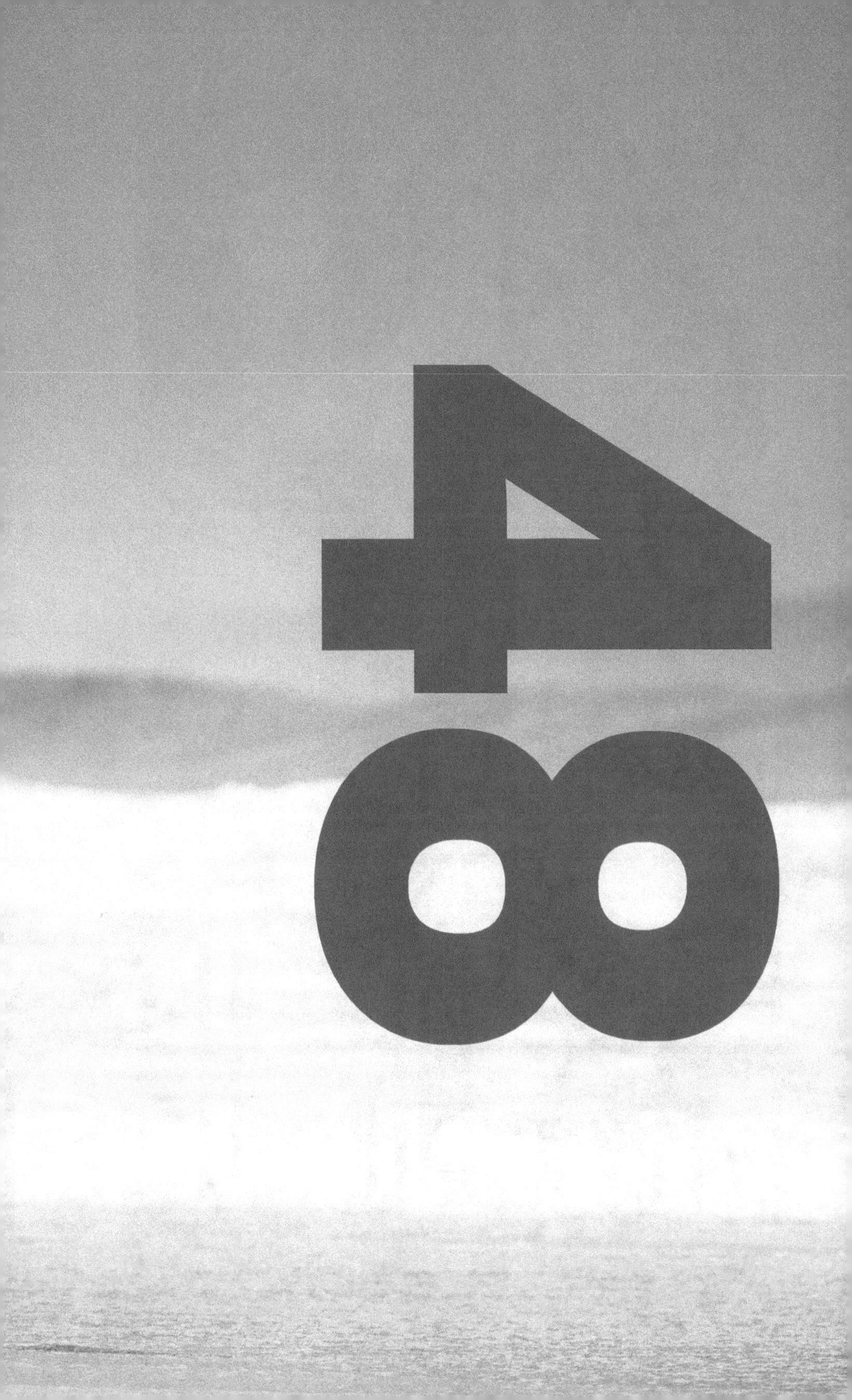

48

TO HIM
WHO IS ABLE
TO KEEP YOU FROM
FALLING
FALLING
AND TO PRESENT YOU
BEFORE HIS
GLORIOUS PRESENCE
WITHOUT FAULT
AND WITH GREAT

JOY

JUDE 24

TO THE ONLY
GOD OUR SAVIOR BE

Glory

MAJESTY

POWER

AND AUTHORITY
THROUGH JESUS CHRIST
OUR LORD,
BEFORE ALL AGES,
NOW AND FOREVERMORE.

Amen

JUDE 25

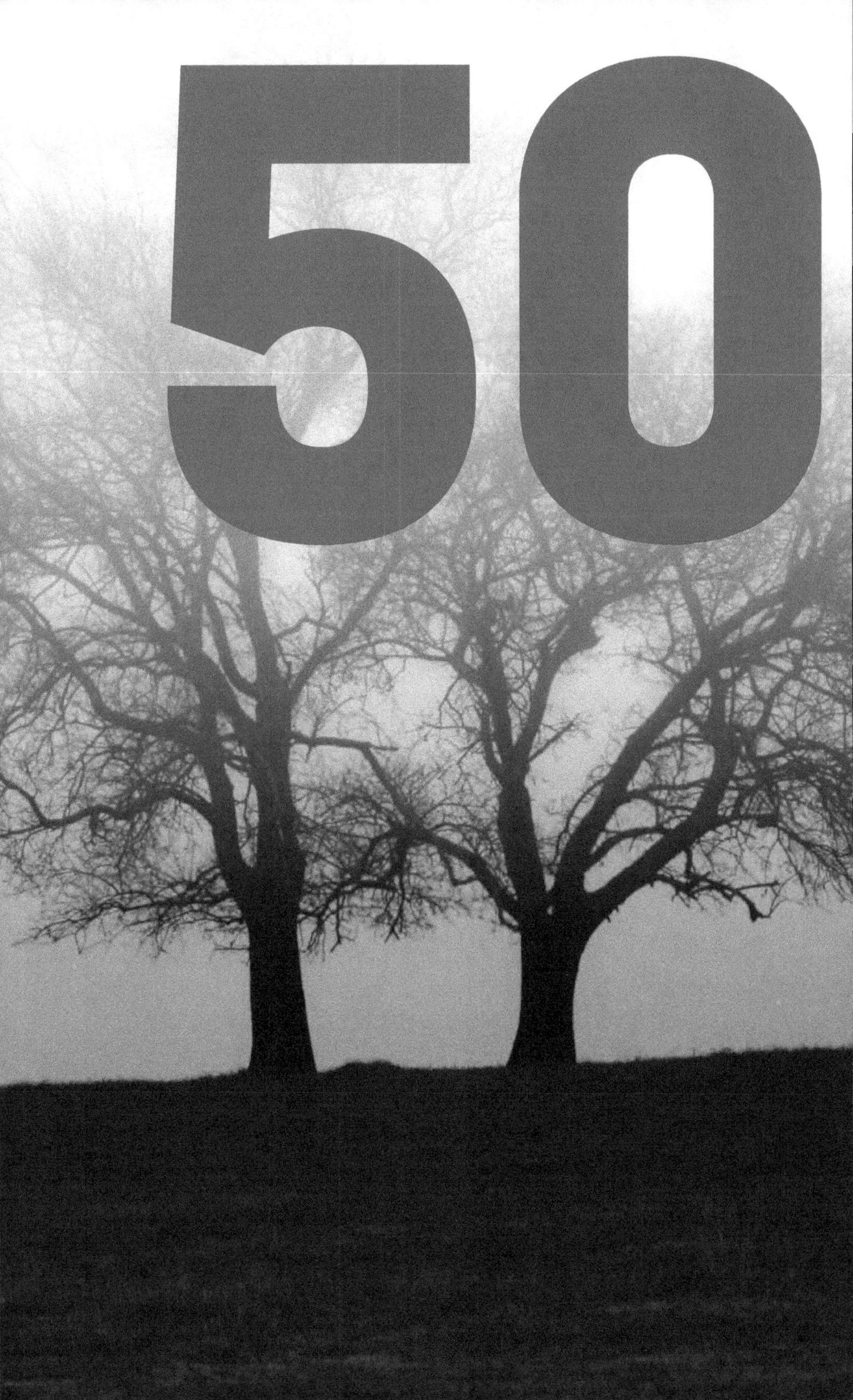
50

DO NOT BE

afraid

I AM THE FIRST
AND THE LAST.
I AM THE LIVING ONE;
I WAS DEAD
AND BEHOLD I AM

Alive

FOREVER AND EVER!

REVELATION 1:17

YOU ARE

Worthy

OUR LORD AND GOD,
TO RECEIVE

GLORY

AND HONOR,
AND POWER,
FOR YOU CREATED ALL THINGS
AND BY YOUR WILL
THEY WERE CREATED
AND HAVE THEIR BEING.

REVELATION 4:11

CPSIA information can be obtained
at www.ICGtesting.com
Printed in the USA
FSHW022225200219
55785FS